I Can Master
Division

Carson-Dellosa Publishing, LLC
Greensboro, North Carolina

Credits

Content Editor: Erin McCarthy
Copy Editor: Julie B. Killian
Layout and Cover Design: Lori Jackson
Cover Illustration: Nick Greenwood

Visit *carsondellosa.com* for correlations to Common Core State, national, and Canadian provincial standards.

Carson-Dellosa Publishing, LLC
PO Box 35665
Greensboro, NC 27425 USA
carsondellosa.com

ISBN 978-1-60996-956-1

Introduction

I Can Master Division is the perfect tool for teachers looking for that extra something to help reluctant and struggling students practice basic facts. This book contains standards-based, fun activities including:

- Mazes
- Hidden pictures
- Number searches
- Riddles
- Codes
- And more!

Copy and cut out the "karate belt" bracelets to use as rewards when students master a set of division facts. Copy and give the award certificate to students who master all of their division facts 1–12.

Table of Contents

CD-104580 • © Carson-Dellosa

Common Core State Standards Supported

Third Grade	
Operations and Algebraic Thinking	
Represent and solve problems involving multiplication and division.	Pages 11, 20, 21, 25, 32, 38
Understand properties of multiplication and the relationship between multiplication and division.	Pages 11, 20, 21, 25, 32, 33, 38
Multiply and divide within 100.	Pages 4–44
Number and Operations in Base Ten	
Use place value understanding and properties of operations to perform multi-digit arithmetic.	Pages 30, 35, 44
Fourth Grade	
Operations and Algebraic Thinking	
Use the four operations with whole numbers to solve problems.	Pages 11, 20, 21, 25, 32, 38
Gain familiarity with factors and multiples.	Pages 4–44
Generate and analyze patterns.	Page 33

Name_____ Date_____

 **Tortoise vs. Hare**

Solve each problem to reach the finish line.

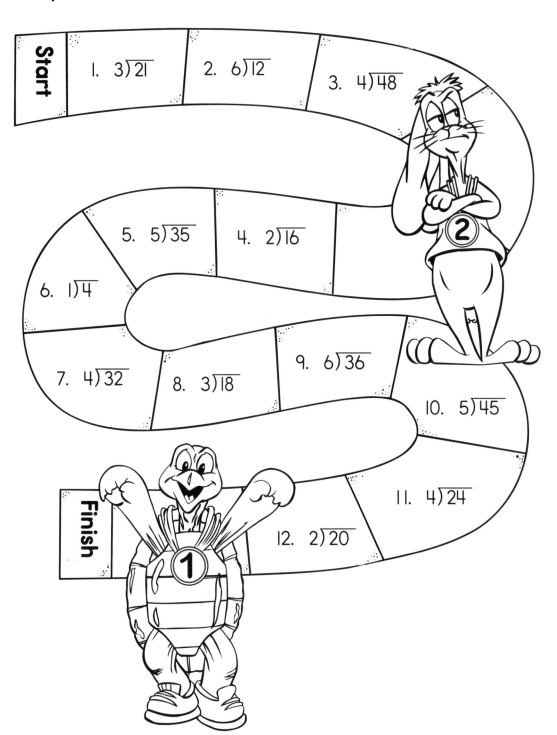

Start

1. $3\overline{)21}$

2. $6\overline{)12}$

3. $4\overline{)48}$

5. $5\overline{)35}$

4. $2\overline{)16}$

6. $1\overline{)4}$

7. $4\overline{)32}$

8. $3\overline{)18}$

9. $6\overline{)36}$

10. $5\overline{)45}$

11. $4\overline{)24}$

12. $2\overline{)20}$

Finish

Wise Owl

Solve each problem. Find and circle the problems in the puzzle and add the correct symbols. Problems can be found across and down. The first one has been done for you.

1. 3 ÷ 3 = __1__

2. 15 ÷ 5 = _____

3. 24 ÷ 6 = _____

4. 25 ÷ 5 = _____

5. 10 ÷ 2 = _____

6. 8 ÷ 4 = _____

7. 9 ÷ 3 = _____

8. 20 ÷ 4 = _____

9. 15 ÷ 3 = _____

10. 4 ÷ 2 = _____

11. 12 ÷ 3 = _____

12. 12 ÷ 6 = _____

13. 5 ÷ 5 = _____

14. 10 ÷ 5 = _____

15. 8 ÷ 2 = _____

16. 6 ÷ 3 = _____

17. 16 ÷ 4 = _____

18. 6 ÷ 2 = _____

1	8	2	4	15	8	12	4	2	2	3
6	1	3	4	10	4	20	9	6	0	7
12	12	4	12	5	1	1	2	2	5	2
3	3	16	6	2	16	15	6	3	8	6
6	4	1	2	1	4	5	9	3	3	1
16	8	4	2	3	4	3	1	9	0	5
7	1	15	3	5	20	2	24	6	4	0
20	16	5	2	25	5	5	7	1	20	10
4	6	3	2	7	9	2	3	5	9	7
5	1	5	1	10	2	5	÷ 3	2	1	14
14	2	12	3	10	4	8	= 1	6	4	5
10	8	2	5	5	1	6	25	8	24	15

Falling Leaf Facts

Solve each problem. Color each leaf with an odd quotient green. Color each leaf with an even quotient yellow.

$9 \div 3 =$

$6 \div 3 =$

$14 \div 2 =$

$15 \div 3 =$

$10 \div 5 =$

$8 \div 1 =$

$16 \div 4 =$

$10 \div 2 =$

$12 \div 6 =$

$6 \div 2 =$

$8 \div 2 =$

$8 \div 4 =$

$12 \div 3 =$

$16 \div 2 =$

Name_____ Date_____

Tic-Tac-Divide

Solve each problem. To find the winner of each game, draw an *O* on each problem with an odd quotient and draw an *X* on each problem with an even quotient.

2)12	6)54	5)55
6)36	4)16	3)9
5)35	1)8	3)6

4)20	2)14	6)18
3)12	5)40	5)45
2)16	6)42	4)24

5)25	6)24	2)10
3)12	5)40	6)36
2)6	5)5	5)20

5)30	1)9	3)3
3)18	2)14	6)36
5)20	3)24	3)21

What's the Secret?

Solve each problem. For each answer, color two spaces in the grid with matching numbers. The colored spaces will reveal a secret message.

1. $6 \div 3 =$ _____

2. $36 \div 6 =$ _____

3. $6 \div 1 =$ _____

4. $12 \div 6 =$ _____

5. $15 \div 5 =$ _____

6. $45 \div 5 =$ _____

7. $24 \div 6 =$ _____

8. $18 \div 6 =$ _____

9. $40 \div 4 =$ _____

10. $16 \div 2 =$ _____

11. $42 \div 6 =$ _____

12. $48 \div 6 =$ _____

13. $30 \div 6 =$ _____

14. $12 \div 3 =$ _____

15. $10 \div 2 =$ _____

16. $60 \div 6 =$ _____

17. $54 \div 6 =$ _____

18. $6 \div 6 =$ _____

19. $28 \div 4 =$ _____

0	2	12	11	16	14	15	13	5	3	6	0	13	11	14	15	11	13	19
19	17	21	0	6	5	10	13	10	14	11	19	7	0	9	11	9	9	7
7	3	2	12	16	13	17	18	1	8	4	21	2	20	4	17	5	13	8
0	11	18	20	10	8	6	0	4	21	12	19	9	17	5	0	10	18	8
11	4	16	15	12	11	13	19	6	14	17	0	3	2	7	18	1	20	3

 **Ice Cream Sundae**

Solve each problem. Use the key to color the picture.

Key

1, 2 = blue   3, 4 = yellow   5, 6 = brown   7, 8 = pink   9, 10 = green

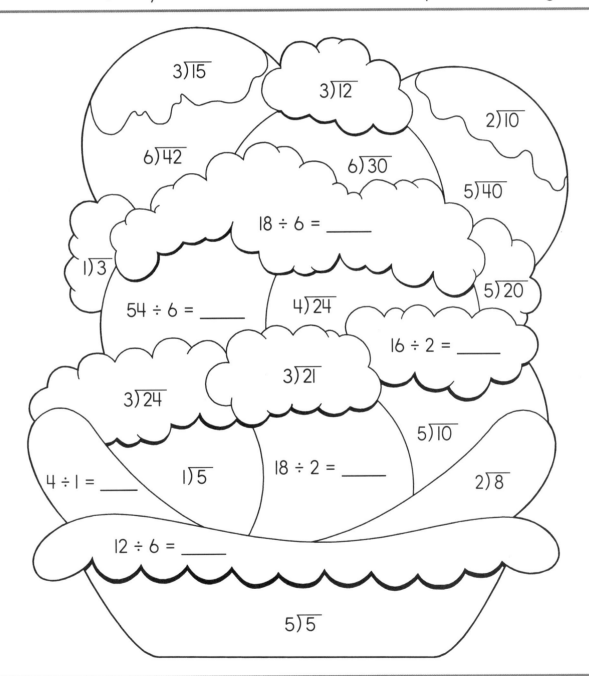

Finding Facts

Solve each problem. Find and circle the problems in the puzzle and add the correct symbols. Problems can be found across and down. The first one has been done for you.

1. $12 \div 2 =$ __6__   2. $12 \div 4 =$ ____   3. $16 \div 4 =$ ____   4. $24 \div 3 =$ ____

5. $42 \div 6 =$ ____   6. $18 \div 6 =$ ____   7. $54 \div 6 =$ ____   8. $21 \div 3 =$ ____

9. $35 \div 5 =$ ____   10. $20 \div 4 =$ ____   11. $48 \div 6 =$ ____   12. $28 \div 4 =$ ____

13. $30 \div 5 =$ ____   14. $15 \div 3 =$ ____   15. $30 \div 6 =$ ____   16. $36 \div 6 =$ ____

17. $25 \div 5 =$ ____   18. $45 \div 5 =$ ____

36	6	7	12	4	3	9	1	16	4	4	15	3
35	4	6	54	3	5	32	3	28	8	36	6	28
5	24	4	6	49	3	36	25	5	49	7	12	4
7	42	7	9	5	21	6	5	18	15	3	5	7
15	3	9	10	36	9	6	5	32	4	16	8	27
36	9	8	27	3	12	8	24	30	6	5	40	9
18	2	7	18	40	5	36	7	20	30	5	4	6
30	21	12	6	4	20	9	30	5	6	20	3	45
27	3	8	3	49	7	24	3	8	28	4	15	5
5	7	42	9	16	2	35	7	18	3	5	30	9
36	7	3	27	3	4	42	6	7	49	7	2	16
4	$12 \div 2 = 6$		16	4	1	14	48	6	8	5	32
2	6	4	5	30	20	7	36	5	40	27	7	2

Animal Antics

Help the boy find the animals that snuck out of the zoo. Draw a line from each problem to its picture to its answer. Write the three letters in order on the line beside the answer. Then, find and circle the animal in the picture. The first one has been done for you.

A. 8 ÷ 2 –

Y. 6 ÷ 3

E. 4 ÷ 2

O. 9 ÷ 3

F. 12 ÷ 2

L. ▪▪   ▪▪

A. ▲ ▲ ▲
   ▲ ▲ ▲

W. ● ● ●
   ● ● ●
   ● ● ●

O. ▲▲▲ ▲▲▲
   ▲▲▲ ▲▲▲

P. ▦ ▦

K. 2_____

L. 3_____

E. 4 __APE__

X. 6_____

K. 2_____

Name_____ Date_____

Petal Problems

Solve each problem. Use the key to color the picture.

Key			
1, 2, 3 = red	4, 5, 6 = yellow	7, 8, 9 = green	10, 11, 12 = orange

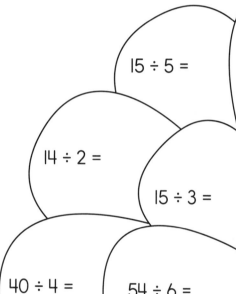
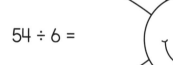

18 ÷ 3 =

15 ÷ 5 =

48 ÷ 6 =

14 ÷ 2 =

27 ÷ 3 =

44 ÷ 4 =

15 ÷ 3 =

9 ÷ 3 =

40 ÷ 4 =

54 ÷ 6 =

18 ÷ 3 =

24 ÷ 3 =

12 ÷ 2 =

22 ÷ 2 =

24 ÷ 4 =

36 ÷ 4 =

35 ÷ 7 =

24 ÷ 2 =

48 ÷ 4 =

6 ÷ 2 =

Digging for Quotients

Solve each problem. Color a bone with a matching quotient. One bone will not be colored.

1. 6 ÷ 2 = _____   2. 4 ÷ 2 = _____

3. 10 ÷ 2 = _____   4. 12 ÷ 2 = _____

5. 12 ÷ 4 = _____   6. 15 ÷ 3 = _____

7. 16 ÷ 4 = _____   8. 6 ÷ 3 = _____

9. 8 ÷ 4 = _____   10. 18 ÷ 2 = _____

11. 15 ÷ 5 = _____   12. 12 ÷ 6 = _____

13. 12 ÷ 3 = _____   14. 7 ÷ 1 = _____

15. 10 ÷ 5 = _____   16. 9 ÷ 3 = _____

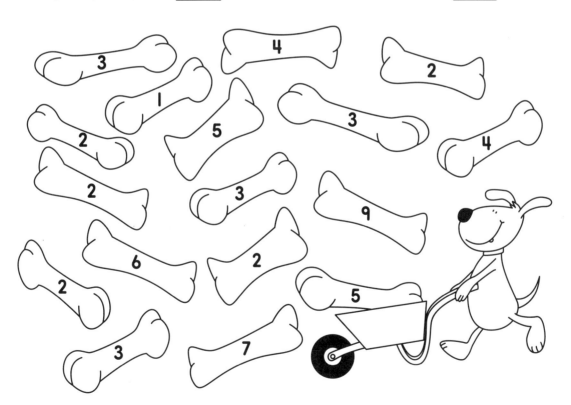

 **Three in a Row**

Solve the problems in each tic-tac-toe game. Circle three problems in a row that have the same answer.

24 ÷ 8 =	54 ÷ 9 =	96 ÷ 12 =
21 ÷ 3 =	64 ÷ 8 =	72 ÷ 9 =
56 ÷ 8 =	32 ÷ 8 =	80 ÷ 10 =

56 ÷ 7 =	8 ÷ 8 =	45 ÷ 9 =
64 ÷ 8 =	64 ÷ 8 =	72 ÷ 9 =
36 ÷ 9 =	28 ÷ 7 =	44 ÷ 11 =

42 ÷ 7 =	108 ÷ 12 =	35 ÷ 7 =
27 ÷ 9 =	48 ÷ 8 =	63 ÷ 9 =
48 ÷ 12 =	40 ÷ 10 =	28 ÷ 7 =

21 ÷ 7 =	24 ÷ 8 =	27 ÷ 9 =
18 ÷ 9 =	63 ÷ 9 =	64 ÷ 8 =
88 ÷ 11 =	56 ÷ 7 =	63 ÷ 7 =

 CD-104580 • © Carson-Dellosa

Hidden Quotients

Solve each problem. Find and circle the problems in the puzzle and add the correct symbols. Problems can be found across and down. The first one has been done for you.

1. 81 ÷ 9 = __9__

2. 40 ÷ 10 = ____

3. 77 ÷ 11 = ____

4. 36 ÷ 12 = ____

5. 80 ÷ 10 = ____

6. 22 ÷ 11 = ____

7. 32 ÷ 8 = ____

8. 84 ÷ 12 = ____

9. 60 ÷ 10 = ____

10. 99 ÷ 11 = ____

11. 48 ÷ 8 = ____

12. 42 ÷ 7 = ____

13. 63 ÷ 7 = ____

14. 56 ÷ 8 = ____

15. 45 ÷ 9 = ____

16. 72 ÷ 9 = ____

17. 60 ÷ 12 = ____

18. 64 ÷ 8 = ____

40	72	22	11	2	8	77	11	7	2
32	36	4	9	3	7	14	1	6	84
40	10	4	9	81	24	63	32	8	12
8	1	45	36	÷	80	4	49	7	7
45	72	9	12	9 = 9	10	30	8	56	4
72	9	5	3	32	8	36	64	21	18
0	8	8	3	8	18	64	8	8	3
56	2	32	6	4	63	16	8	24	6
8	45	63	7	9	42	7	6	4	42
7	2	60	12	5	6	15	60	10	6
3	99	11	9	4	8	64	48	8	6

Software Fun

Solve each problem. To solve the riddle, match the quotients to the letters in the key and write the letters in order on the lines.

Why did the computer buy glasses?

Key

1 = R	2 = P	3 = O	4 = T	5 = W	6 = B
7 = E	8 = G	9 = I	10 = M	11 = V	12 = S

1. 28 ÷ 7 = _____

2. 30 ÷ 10 = _____

3. 108 ÷ 12 = _____

4. 70 ÷ 7 = _____

5. 24 ÷ 12 = _____

6. 11 ÷ 11 = _____

7. 27 ÷ 9 = _____

8. 121 ÷ 11 = _____

9. 63 ÷ 9 = _____

10. 99 ÷ 11 = _____

11. 32 ÷ 8 = _____

12. 84 ÷ 7 = _____

13. 50 ÷ 10 = _____

14. 49 ÷ 7 = _____

15. 72 ÷ 12 = _____

16. 144 ÷ 12 = _____

17. 72 ÷ 8 = _____

18. 56 ÷ 7 = _____

19. 36 ÷ 9 = _____

Answer: ____ ____

__ __ __ __ __ __ __ __

__ __ __

__ __ __ - __ __ __ __ H __

Parallel Parking

Solve each problem. To solve the riddle, match the quotients to the letters in the key and write the letters in order on the lines.

Key					
1 = R	2 = O	3 = A	4 = E	5 = P	6 = N
7 = T	8 = K	9 = I	10 = S	11 = G	12 = M

1. $7\overline{)21}$

2. $9\overline{)63}$

3. $8\overline{)40}$

4. $12\overline{)36}$

5. $8\overline{)8}$

6. $10\overline{)80}$

7. $7\overline{)63}$

8. $12\overline{)72}$

9. $11\overline{)121}$

10. $9\overline{)108}$

11. $8\overline{)32}$

12. $12\overline{)84}$

13. $9\overline{)36}$

14. $9\overline{)18}$

15. $12\overline{)12}$

16. $11\overline{)110}$

Where do astronauts park their spacecraft?

Answer: ____ ____   ____ ____ ____ ____ ____ ____

" ____ ____ ____ ____ ____ ____ ____ "

In Flight

Solve each problem. Use the key to color the picture.

Key				
0, 1 = blue	2, 3 = brown	4, 5 = green	6, 7 = black	8 = yellow

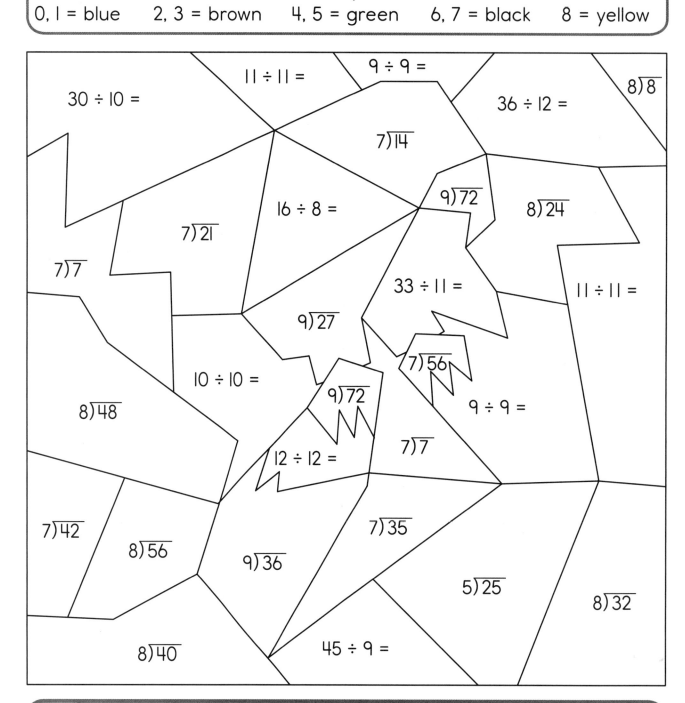

$30 \div 10 =$

$11 \div 11 =$

$9 \div 9 =$

$8)\overline{8}$

$36 \div 12 =$

$7)\overline{14}$

$16 \div 8 =$

$7)\overline{21}$

$9)\overline{72}$

$8)\overline{24}$

$7)\overline{7}$

$33 \div 11 =$

$11 \div 11 =$

$9)\overline{27}$

$10 \div 10 =$

$7)\overline{56}$

$9)\overline{72}$

$9 \div 9 =$

$8)\overline{48}$

$12 \div 12 =$

$7)\overline{7}$

$7)\overline{42}$

$8)\overline{56}$

$9)\overline{36}$

$7)\overline{35}$

$5)\overline{25}$

$8)\overline{32}$

$8)\overline{40}$

$45 \div 9 =$

CD-104580 • © Carson-Dellosa

 **Riddle Time**

Solve each set of problems. To solve each riddle, write the corresponding letters in order from least to greatest quotient.

1. What can you wear any time that never goes out of style?

77 ÷ 11 =	81 ÷ 9 =	8 ÷ 8 =	80 ÷ 8 =	48 ÷ 12 =	84 ÷ 7 =
M	I	A	L	S	E

2. What goes up but never comes down?

96 ÷ 8 =	24 ÷ 8 =	132 ÷ 12 =	63 ÷ 7 =	22 ÷ 11 =	30 ÷ 6 =	63 ÷ 9 =
E	O	G	A	Y	U	R

3. What go up and down but do not move?

28 ÷ 7 =	81 ÷ 9 =	36 ÷ 12 =	54 ÷ 9 =	108 ÷ 9 =	56 ÷ 7 =
T	R	S	A	S	I

 **Picturing Division**

Draw a line from each problem to its array.

45 ÷ 9

14 ÷ 7

40 ÷ 8

49 ÷ 7

9 ÷ 9

18 ÷ 9

64 ÷ 8

16 ÷ 8

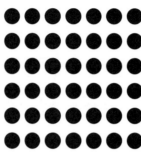

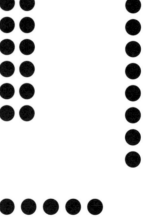

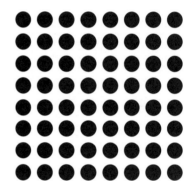
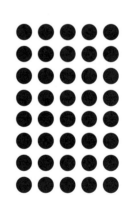

Grid Pattern

Solve each problem. For each answer, color the space on the grid with the matching number. The colored spaces will reveal a pattern.

1. [ ] ÷ 7 = 9

2. [ ] ÷ 9 = 9

3. [ ] ÷ 7 = 2

4. 45 ÷ 9 = [ ]

5. 14 ÷ 7 = [ ]

6. 99 ÷ 9 = [ ]

7. [ ] ÷ 9 = 6

8. [ ] ÷ 7 = 7

9. 56 ÷ 7 = [ ]

10. [ ] ÷ 8 = 8

2	3	1	4
10	5	6	7
16	17	8	9
19	24	12	11
20	36	14	21
18	81	23	22
64	26	27	28
30	49	32	33
45	40	54	47
61	55	57	63

"Hay" There!

Solve each problem. Use the key to color the picture.

Key
1 = red   2, 3 = green   4 = yellow   5, 6 = black   7, 8, 9 = brown

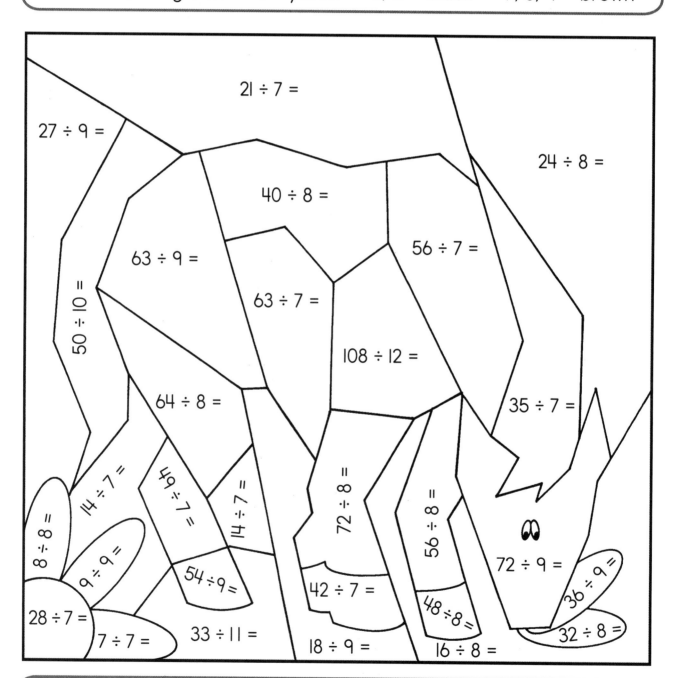

Oddly Enough

Solve each problem. Color each space with an odd quotient blue. Color each space with an even quotient green. The picture will solve the riddle.

What letter of the alphabet is also a drink?

$9\overline{)18}$	$8\overline{)24}$	$9\overline{)63}$	$12\overline{)60}$	$10\overline{)30}$	$7\overline{)35}$	$9\overline{)9}$	$7\overline{)28}$
$10\overline{)60}$	$12\overline{)84}$	$8\overline{)72}$	$7\overline{)63}$	$10\overline{)70}$	$11\overline{)99}$	$9\overline{)45}$	$12\overline{)48}$
$12\overline{)72}$	$11\overline{)110}$	$8\overline{)48}$	$8\overline{)40}$	$7\overline{)49}$	$9\overline{)54}$	$8\overline{)64}$	$7\overline{)42}$
$12\overline{)24}$	$11\overline{)88}$	$7\overline{)56}$	$7\overline{)21}$	$9\overline{)81}$	$10\overline{)40}$	$8\overline{)32}$	$7\overline{)70}$
$9\overline{)36}$	$8\overline{)96}$	$11\overline{)66}$	$10\overline{)90}$	$12\overline{)36}$	$10\overline{)100}$	$8\overline{)80}$	$9\overline{)72}$
$10\overline{)20}$	$12\overline{)96}$	$7\overline{)84}$	$8\overline{)56}$	$9\overline{)27}$	$12\overline{)120}$	$10\overline{)80}$	$11\overline{)44}$
$7\overline{)14}$	$9\overline{)90}$	$11\overline{)22}$	$11\overline{)77}$	$12\overline{)108}$	$8\overline{)16}$	$12\overline{)144}$	$10\overline{)120}$

Name_____   Date_____

Fluttering Facts

Solve each problem. Use the key to color the picture.

Key

2 = brown   5 = purple   6 = green   7 = orange   8 = yellow   9 = black

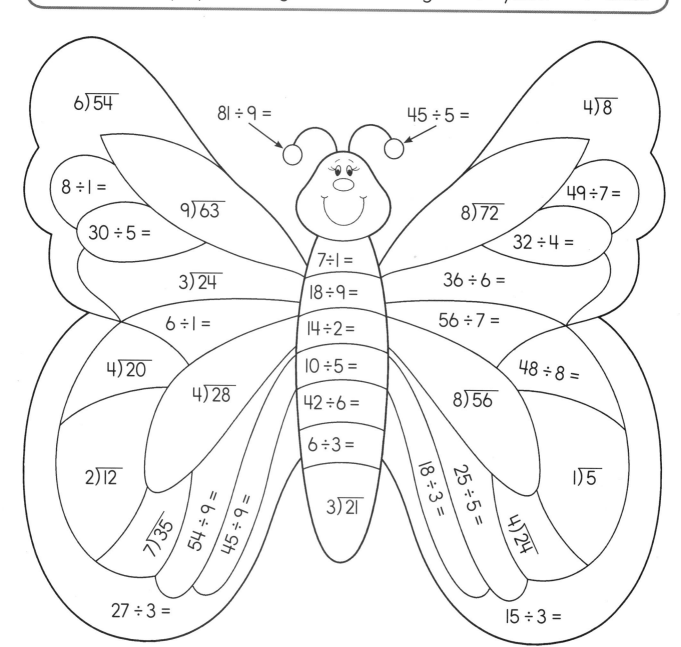

 # Dot-to-Dot Division

Solve each set of problems from top to bottom. Connect the dots in the order of your answers, beginning with the given number.

A. Start at 6

$30 \div \underline{} = 6$ $6 \div \underline{} = 1$

$15 \div \underline{} = 5$ $21 \div \underline{} = 7$

$28 \div \underline{} = 4$ $40 \div \underline{} = 5$

$20 \div \underline{} = 4$ $48 \div \underline{} = 8$

$9 \div \underline{} = 9$

$56 \div \underline{} = 8$

```
        2
        •
 3•          •5

8•             •1

 6•          •7
        •
        4
```

B. Start at 2

$5 \div \underline{} = 5$ $45 \div \underline{} = 9$

$63 \div \underline{} = 9$ $12 \div \underline{} = 4$

$9 \div \underline{} = 3$ $21 \div \underline{} = 3$

$8 \div \underline{} = 4$ $63 \div \underline{} = 7$

$18 \div \underline{} = 3$ $25 \div \underline{} = 5$

$56 \div \underline{} = 7$

```
        7
        •
 1•          •9

8•             •6

 5•          •2
        •
        3
```

C. Start at 5

$45 \div \underline{} = 5$ $24 \div \underline{} = 8$

$12 \div \underline{} = 6$ $42 \div \underline{} = 7$

$36 \div \underline{} = 6$ $6 \div \underline{} = 3$

$6 \div \underline{} = 2$ $27 \div \underline{} = 3$

$8 \div \underline{} = 1$ $2 \div \underline{} = 2$

$35 \div \underline{} = 7$ $54 \div \underline{} = 9$

$7 \div \underline{} = 1$

```
        7
        •
 2•          •3

9•             •6

 5•          •1
        •
        8
```

Climbing to the Top

Start at the bottom of the stairs. Find the quotient for the first problem. Use that quotient as the divisor for the next step. Repeat until you reach the top.

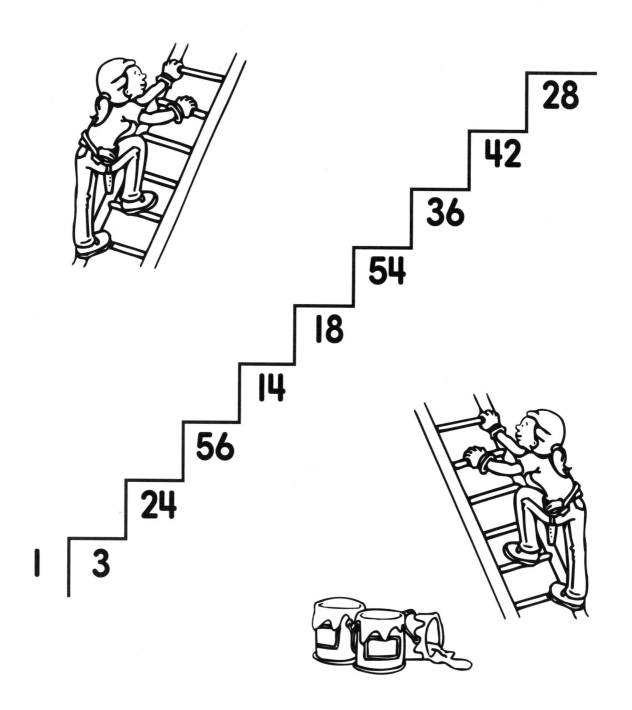

28

42

36

54

18

14

56

24

1 | 3

Odd or Even?

Solve each problem. To find the winner of each game, draw an **O** on each problem with an odd quotient and draw an **X** on each problem with an even quotient.

$5\overline{)10}$	$4\overline{)8}$	$24 \div 4 =$
$4\overline{)36}$	$35\overline{)5}$	$4\overline{)32}$
$45 \div 5 =$	$5\overline{)30}$	$4\overline{)12}$

$28 \div 4 =$	$5\overline{)30}$	$45 \div 5 =$
$4\overline{)16}$	$32 \div 4 =$	$5\overline{)15}$
$20 \div 4 =$	$12 \div 3 =$	$4\overline{)8}$

$5\overline{)25}$	$8 \div 4 =$	$4\overline{)16}$
$32 \div 4 =$	$5\overline{)20}$	$5\overline{)35}$
$5\overline{)40}$	$4\overline{)12}$	$15 \div 5 =$

$36 \div 12 =$	$9\overline{)18}$	$7\overline{)42}$
$2\overline{)12}$	$45 \div 9 =$	$64 \div 8 =$
$9\overline{)81}$	$24 \div 6 =$	$7\overline{)49}$

Number Word Puzzle

Solve each problem. Write the number word for each answer in the puzzle. The first one has been done for you.

Across	Down
1. 42 ÷ 7 = **6**	1. 49 ÷ 7 =
2. 30 ÷ 6 =	2. 36 ÷ 9 =
3. 16 ÷ 8 =	3. 12 ÷ 1 =
4. 66 ÷ 6 =	5. 80 ÷ 8 =
5. 12 ÷ 4 =	6. 24 ÷ 3 =
8. 45 ÷ 5 =	7. 2 ÷ 2 =

Catch-a-Fact

Solve each problem. Find and circle the problems in the puzzle and add the correct symbols. Problems can be found across and down. The first one has been done for you.

1. $72 \div 9 = $ __8__

2. $64 \div 8 = $ ____

3. $28 \div 7 = $ ____

4. $48 \div 6 = $ ____

5. $18 \div 9 = $ ____

6. $30 \div 5 = $ ____

7. $42 \div 7 = $ ____

8. $36 \div 9 = $ ____

9. $32 \div 8 = $ ____

10. $6 \div 1 = $ ____

11. $56 \div 8 = $ ____

12. $12 \div 2 = $ ____

13. $54 \div 6 = $ ____

14. $9 \div 1 = $ ____

15. $8 \div 1 = $ ____

16. $20 \div 5 = $ ____

17. $40 \div 8 = $ ____

18. $3 \div 1 = $ ____

(72÷9=8)	5	1	0	0	54	10	27	3	9	8	9	48
3	6	18	20	6	5	9	6	21	7	68	10	15	1	6
56	8	7	4	1	16	40	9	55	42	7	6	3	9	8
45	7	16	0	6	8	8	5	33	35	2	24	3	7	3
4	9	32	8	4	2	5	9	0	0	16	20	5	4	18
3	5	17	0	3	64	72	1	14	8	74	21	1	64	2
1	10	18	9	2	8	20	6	8	1	8	13	32	5	9
3	0	70	10	7	8	0	18	2	12	0	12	2	6	81
22	65	17	5	11	20	27	36	9	4	5	41	19	61	0
17	1	7	2	38	36	28	4	7	12	42	28	7	4	36
30	5	6	50	13	45	18	45	52	9	3	3	5	45	60

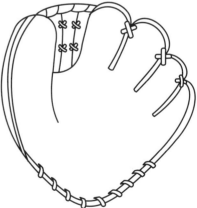

 **Jersey Division**

Use the digits on each jersey to complete the division problem. The first one has been done for you.

1.

2.

3.

4.

5.

6.

7.

8.

9.

10.

11.

12.

Name_____ Date_____ Division Facts 1-9

 **Time to Divide**

Solve each problem. To solve the riddle, match the numbers and write the letters on the lines.

Why did the boy throw the clock out the window?

1. 16 ÷ 8 = ____ **D**   6. 81 ÷ 9 = ____ **I**

2. 56 ÷ 7 = ____ **O**   7. 32 ÷ 8 = ____ **N**

3. 99 ÷ 9 = ____ **A**   8. 48 ÷ 8 = ____ **M**

4. 77 ÷ 11 = ____ **L**   9. 21 ÷ 7 = ____ **W**

5. 45 ÷ 9 = ____ **T**

Answer:

H E ___ ___ ___ ___ E ___   ___ ___ S E E
     3   11 4   5   2   5   8

___ ___ ___ E   F ___ Y!
5   9   6   7

Name_____ Date_____

The Ball Drops

Solve the first problem in each column. Drop the answer to the ball below and solve to complete the next ball. Continue until you have completed all of the equations.

Column 1

$64 \div 8 = \bigcirc$

$\bigcirc \div 3 = \bigcirc$

$\bigcirc \div \bigcirc = 6$

$20 \div \bigcirc = \bigcirc$

$35 \div \bigcirc = \bigcirc$

$14 \div \bigcirc = \bigcirc$

$\bigcirc \div 6 = \bigcirc$

$\bigcirc \div \bigcirc = 4$

$27 \div \bigcirc = \bigcirc$

$\bigcirc \div 6 = \bigcirc$

Column 2

$3 \div \bigcirc = 1$

$\bigcirc \div \bigcirc = 6$

$\bigcirc \div 9 = \bigcirc$

$\bigcirc \div 8 = \bigcirc$

$\bigcirc \div \bigcirc = 4$

$28 \div \bigcirc = \bigcirc$

$21 \div \bigcirc = \bigcirc$

$15 \div \bigcirc = \bigcirc$

$40 \div \bigcirc = \bigcirc$

$\bigcirc \div \bigcirc = 9$

Column 3

$8 \div \bigcirc = 4$

$10 \div \bigcirc = \bigcirc$

$45 \div \bigcirc = \bigcirc$

$81 \div \bigcirc = \bigcirc$

$63 \div \bigcirc = \bigcirc$

$49 \div \bigcirc = \bigcirc$

$42 \div \bigcirc = \bigcirc$

$\bigcirc \div \bigcirc = 6$

$\bigcirc \div \bigcirc = 4$

$\bigcirc \div \bigcirc = 3$

Homework Machines

Use the rule at the beginning of each machine to complete the bulbs.

1.
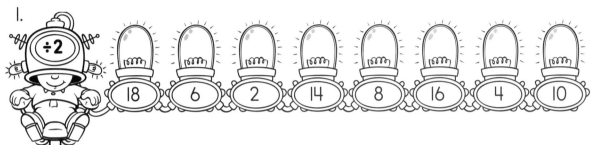

÷2   18   6   2   14   8   16   4   10

2.

18   54   81   9   27   63   36   72   ÷9

3.

÷6   6   30   54   12   24   48   42   18

4.
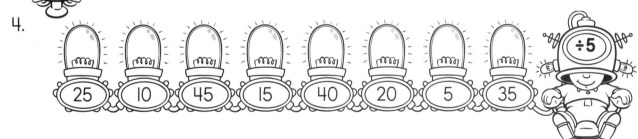

25   10   45   15   40   20   5   35   ÷5

5.

÷8   48   40   64   16   32   8   56   24

Quotient Rows

Solve each problem. To find the winner of each game, draw an O on each problem with an odd quotient and draw an X on each problem with an even quotient.

$4\overline{)36}$	$4\overline{)24}$	$10 \div 5 =$
$5\overline{)40}$	$32 \div 4 =$	$25 \div 5 =$
$35 \div 5 =$	$20 \div 4 =$	$12 \div 4 =$

$4\overline{)32}$	$12 \div 4 =$	$5\overline{)30}$
$4\overline{)28}$	$4\overline{)20}$	$20 \div 4 =$
$20 \div 5 =$	$10 \div 5 =$	$15 \div 5 =$

$25 \div 5 =$	$4\overline{)8}$	$16 \div 4 =$
$32 \div 4 =$	$5\overline{)20}$	$5\overline{)35}$
$40 \div 5 =$	$4\overline{)12}$	$15 \div 5 =$

$5\overline{)10}$	$4\overline{)8}$	$24 \div 4 =$
$4\overline{)36}$	$5\overline{)35}$	$4\overline{)32}$
$45 \div 5 =$	$5\overline{)30}$	$4\overline{)12}$

 **Make-a-Score**

Use the digits on each soccer ball to complete the division problem. The first one has been done for you.

1.

794

$\underline{49} \div \underline{\ 7\ } = 7$

2.

819

$\underline{\ \ \ } \div \underline{\ \ \ } = 2$

3.

972

$\underline{\ \ \ } \div \underline{\ \ \ } = 3$

4.

423

$\underline{\ \ \ } \div \underline{\ \ \ } = 8$

5.

554

$\underline{\ \ \ } \div \underline{\ \ \ } = 9$

6.

804

$\underline{\ \ \ } \div \underline{\ \ \ } = 5$

7.

376

$\underline{\ \ \ } \div \underline{\ \ \ } = 9$

8.

663

$\underline{\ \ \ } \div \underline{\ \ \ } = 6$

9.

274

$\underline{\ \ \ } \div \underline{\ \ \ } = 6$

10.

1428

$\underline{\ \ \ } \div \underline{\ \ \ } = 4$

11.

1881

$\underline{\ \ \ } \div \underline{\ \ \ } = 8$

12.

4100

$\underline{\ \ \ } \div \underline{\ \ \ } = 4$

 **A Different Tune**

Solve each problem. To solve the riddle, match the quotients to the letters in the key and write the letters in order on the lines.

Key					
1 = W	2 = D	3 = G	4 = F	5 = O	6 = H
7 = T	8 = R	9 = Y	10 = E	11 = S	

1. $21 \div 3 =$

2. $18 \div 3 =$

3. $40 \div 4 =$

4. $45 \div 5 =$

5. $24 \div 6 =$

6. $50 \div 10 =$

7. $72 \div 9 =$

8. $36 \div 12 =$

9. $45 \div 9 =$

10. $56 \div 8 =$

11. $77 \div 11 =$

12. $54 \div 9 =$

13. $70 \div 7 =$

14. $11 \div 11 =$

15. $10 \div 2 =$

16. $64 \div 8 =$

17. $16 \div 8 =$

18. $132 \div 12 =$

Why do bees hum?

Answer: BECAUSE ___ ___ ___ ___ ___   ___ ___ ___ ___ ___ ___ ___

___ ___ ___   ___ ___ ___ ___ ___

I Spy

Cut out the puzzle pieces. Arrange the pieces so that each division fact is above its answer. On another sheet of paper, glue the pieces together to reveal a secret picture.

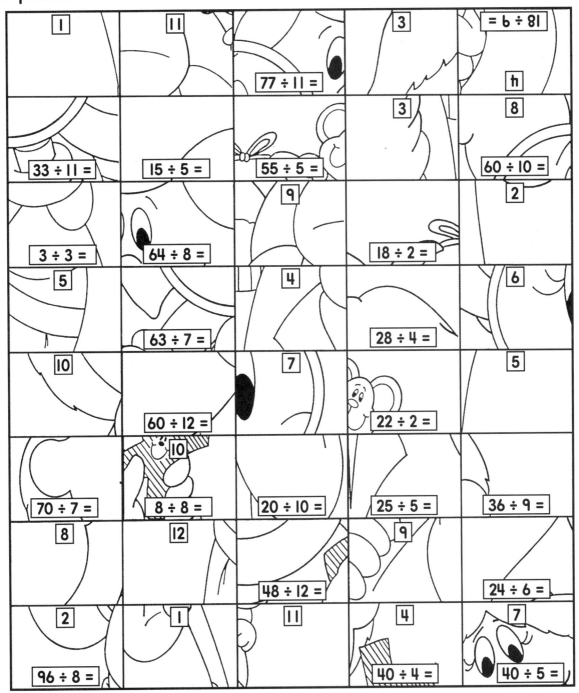

Treasure Hunt

Solve each problem to get to the treasure.

1.

15 ÷

40 ÷

30 ÷

25 ÷

= 5

10 ÷

45 ÷

Treasure

2.

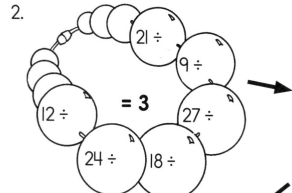

21 ÷

9 ÷

12 ÷

= 3

27 ÷

24 ÷

18 ÷

3.

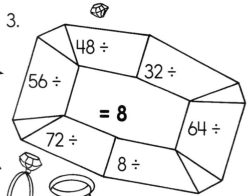

48 ÷

56 ÷

32 ÷

= 8

72 ÷

64 ÷

8 ÷

4.

24 ÷

48 ÷

12 ÷

18 ÷

30 ÷

36 ÷

54 ÷

= 6

5.

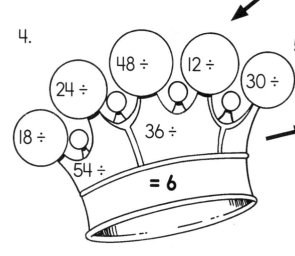

12 ÷

= 2

16 ÷

10 ÷

6 ÷

8 ÷

14 ÷

18 ÷

 ## A Head Above the Rest

Solve each problem. Use the key to color the picture. The picture will solve the riddle.

Key

| 1, 2, 3 = brown | 4, 5, 6 = yellow | 7, 8 = red | 9, 10 = green | 11, 12 = blue |

What has one head, one foot, and four legs?

$54 \div 9 =$ ____

$12 \div 3 =$ ____

$5 \div 5 =$ ____

$40 \div 8 =$ ____

$28 \div 4 =$ ____

$48 \div 6 =$ ____

$16 \div 4 =$ ____

$56 \div 8 =$ ____

$60 \div 5 =$ ____

$55 \div 5 =$ ____

$77 \div 7 =$ ____

$18 \div 6 =$ ____

$36 \div 3 =$ ____

$14 \div 7 =$ ____

$100 \div 10 =$ ____

$81 \div 9 =$ ____

$108 \div 12 =$ ____

$110 \div 11 =$ ____

Name_____ Date_____

Fruity Division

Use the code to solve each problem.

Code

0 = 🍍   1 = 🍌   2 = 🍎   3 = 🍇   4 = 🍊

5 = 🍉   6 = 🍓   7 = 🍐   8 = 🍋   9 = 🍒

1. 🍎 🍍 ÷ 🍉 = _____
2. 🍒 🍍 ÷ 🍌 🍍 = _____
3. 🍌 🍎 ÷ 🍎 = _____
4. 🍇 🍓 ÷ 🍊 = _____
5. 🍌 🍋 ÷ 🍇 = _____
6. 🍋 🍊 ÷ 🍌 🍎 = _____
7. 🍒 ÷ 🍌 = _____
8. 🍊 🍎 ÷ 🍓 = _____

9. 🍊 🍒 ÷ 🍐 = _____
10. 🍓 🍊 ÷ 🍋 = _____
11. 🍇 🍇 ÷ 🍌 🍌 = _____
12. 🍉 🍊 ÷ 🍒 = _____
13. 🍎 🍍 ÷ 🍎 = _____
14. 🍇 🍎 ÷ 🍋 = _____
15. 🍉 🍊 ÷ 🍓 = _____
16. 🍒 🍓 ÷ 🍌 🍎 = _____

Say Cheese!

Draw a line through the path of correctly solved problems to help the mouse find the cheese.

$45 \div 5 = 9$ $72 \div 6 = 12$ $21 \div 3 = 8$

$36 \div 6 = 5$ $24 \div 4 = 6$ $25 \div 5 = 6$

$36 \div 4 = 6$

$2 \div 2 = 4$

$90 \div 10 = 10$ $12 \div 1 = 1$

$42 \div 7 = 7$ $64 \div 8 = 8$

$9 \div 3 = 3$

$12 \div 2 = 6$ $21 \div 7 = 3$ $54 \div 9 = 6$ $77 \div 11 = 17$

$84 \div 12 = 7$

$24 \div 12 = 3$ $72 \div 9 = 7$ $50 \div 5 = 5$

$44 \div 11 = 4$ $6 \div 1 = 6$ $27 \div 3 = 9$ $20 \div 10 = 12$

$6 \div 6 = 6$

$16 \div 8 = 8$ $70 \div 10 = 7$ $12 \div 4 = 8$

$56 \div 7 = 7$ $22 \div 11 = 2$ $32 \div 8 = 4$

Matching Quotients

Draw lines to connect division facts that have the same quotients. To solve the riddle, fill in the boxes with the letters that are intersected by two lines.

What type of clothing does a house wear?

2 ÷ 2

6 ÷ 3

3 ÷ 1

12 ÷ 3

50 ÷ 10

30 ÷ 5

14 ÷ 2

48 ÷ 6

81 ÷ 9

30 ÷ 3

A

D

R

P

E

L

S

14 ÷ 7

24 ÷ 6

8 ÷ 8

27 ÷ 9

72 ÷ 12

56 ÷ 8

20 ÷ 4

63 ÷ 7

10 ÷ 1

88 ÷ 11

Name_____ Date_____

Walking Home

Draw a line through the path of correctly solved problems to help the girl get home.

$32 \div 4 = 8$ $16 \div 8 = 2$ $54 \div 9 = 6$ $27 \div 3 = 9$

$96 \div 12 = 32$ $20 \div 5 = 11$ $45 \div 9 = 5$

$10 \div 2 = 9$

$55 \div 11 = 5$ $60 \div 12 = 5$ $90 \div 10 = 9$ $42 \div 7 = 6$ $32 \div 8 = 9$

$6 \div 1 = 9$ $28 \div 7 = 3$ $11 \div 1 = 10$ $63 \div 8 = 9$

$40 \div 5 = 9$ $15 \div 3 = 10$ $30 \div 6 = 6$

$36 \div 6 = 6$

$18 \div 2 = 9$ $40 \div 10 = 30$ $33 \div 11 = 13$

$21 \div 3 = 7$ $64 \div 8 = 8$

Arranging Numbers

Follow the directions to create division problems.

Example: Arrange the digits 3, 3, 1, and 1 to create a division problem with a quotient of 3.

$$33 \div 11 = 3$$

1. Arrange the digits 3, 4, and 6 to create a division problem with a quotient of 9.

    _____

2. Arrange the digits 3, 5, and 5 to create a division problem with a quotient of 7.

    _____

3. Arrange the digits 1, 5, and 5 to create a division problem with a quotient of 3.

    _____

4. Arrange the even digits 4, 4, 1, and 1 to create a division problem with a quotient of 4.

    _____

5. Arrange the consecutive digits 2, 4, and 8 to create a division problem with a quotient of 3.

    _____

6. Arrange the even digits 4, 5, and 6 to create a division problem with a quotient of 9.

    _____

7. Arrange the consecutive digits 7, 3, and 5 to create a division problem with a quotient of 5.

    _____

8. Arrange the digits 9, 7, and 2 to create a division problem with a quotient of 8.

    _____

"Karate Belt" Bracelet Patterns

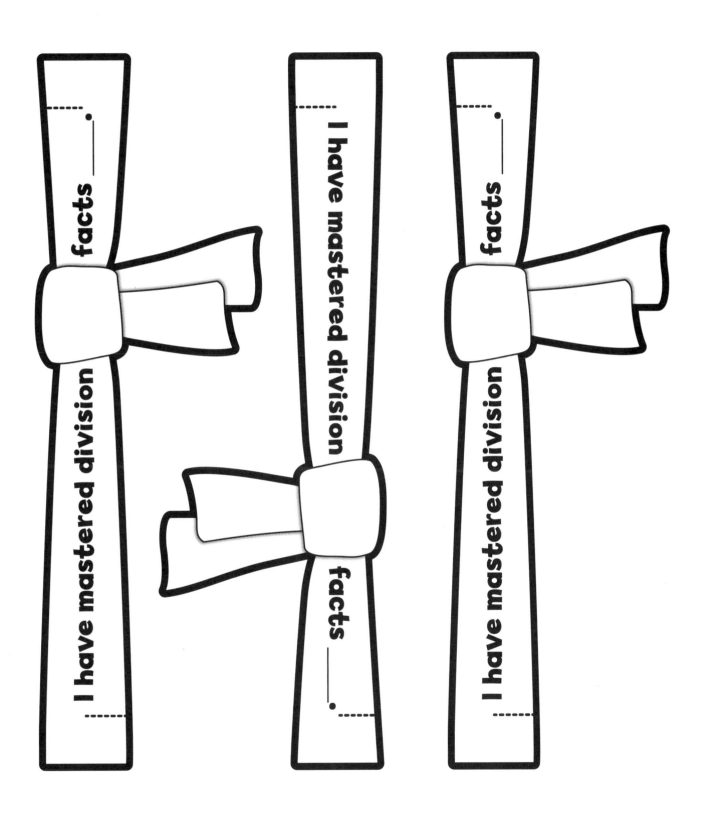

Certified MATH MASTER!

congratulations!

_____

is a master of division facts 1-12.

Page 4

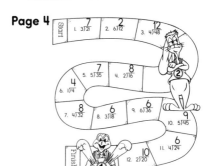

Page 5

1. 1; 2. 3; 3. 4; 4. 5; 5. 5; 6. 2; 7. 3; 8. 5; 9. 5; 10. 2; 11. 4; 12. 2; 13. 1; 14. 2; 15. 4; 16. 2; 17. 4; 18. 3

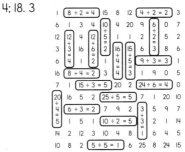

Page 6

Check students' pictures.

Page 7

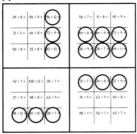

Page 8

1. 2; 2. 6; 3. 6; 4. 2; 5. 3; 6. 9; 7. 4; 8. 3; 9. 10; 10. 8; 11. 7; 12. 8; 13. 5; 14. 4; 15. 5; 16. 10; 17. 9; 18. 1; 19. 7

Secret message: ÷ = Fun

Page 9

Check students' pictures.

Page 10

1. 6; 2. 3; 3. 4; 4. 8; 5. 7; 6. 3; 7. 9; 8. 7; 9. 7; 10. 5; 11. 8; 12. 7; 13. 6; 14. 5; 15. 5; 16. 6; 17. 5; 18. 9

Page 11

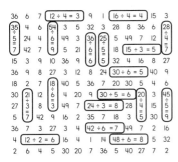

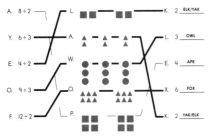

Page 12

Check students' pictures.

Page 13

The number 1 bone will be left uncolored.

Page 14

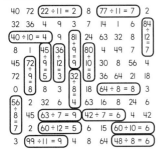

Page 15

1. 9; 2. 4; 3. 7; 4. 3; 5. 8; 6. 2; 7. 4; 8. 7; 9. 6; 10. 9; 11. 6; 12. 6; 13. 9; 14. 7; 15. 5; 16. 8; 17. 5; 18. 8

Page 16

1. 4; 2. 3; 3. 9; 4. 10; 5. 2; 6. 1; 7. 3; 8. 11; 9. 7; 10. 9; 11. 4; 12. 12; 13. 5; 14. 7; 15. 6; 16. 12; 17. 9; 18. 8; 19. 4

Answer: TO IMPROVE ITS WEB-SIGHT

Page 17

1. 3; 2. 7; 3. 5; 4. 3; 5. 1; 6. 8; 7. 9; 8. 6; 9. 11; 10. 12; 11. 4; 12. 7; 13. 4; 14. 2; 15. 1; 16. 10

Answer: AT PARKING "METEORS"

Page 18

Check students' pictures.

Page 19

1. A SMILE; 2. YOUR AGE; 3. STAIRS

Page 20

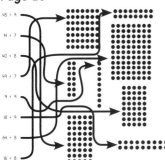

Page 21

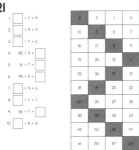

Page 22

Check students' pictures.

Page 23

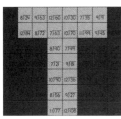

Page 24

Check students' pictures.

Page 25

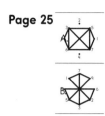

Page 26

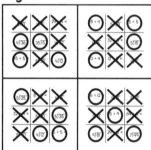

Page 27

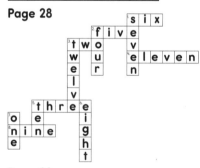

Page 28

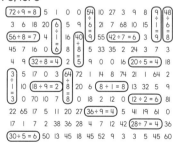

Page 29

1. 8; 2. 8; 3. 4; 4. 8; 5. 2; 6. 6; 7. 6; 8. 4; 9. 4; 10. 6; 11. 7; 12. 6; 13. 9; 14. 9; 15. 8; 16. 4; 17. 5; 18. 3

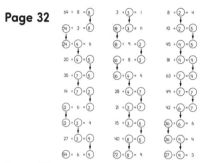

Page 30

1. 21 ÷ 7 = 3; 2. 48 ÷ 4 = 12; 3. 27 ÷ 9 = 3; 4. 48 ÷ 8 = 6; 5. 18 ÷ 9 = 2; 6. 33 ÷ 3 = 11; 7. 42 ÷ 7 = 6; 8. 56 ÷ 8 = 7; 9. 49 ÷ 7 = 7; 10. 63 ÷ 7 = 9; 11. 90 ÷ 9 = 10; 12. 40 ÷ 8 = 5

Page 31

1. 2; 2. 8; 3. 11; 4. 7; 5. 5; 6. 9; 7. 4; 8. 6; 9. 3

Answer: HE WANTED TO SEE TIME FLY!

Page 32

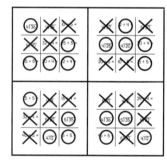

Page 33

1. 9, 3, 1, 7, 4, 8, 2, 5; 2. 2, 6, 9, 1, 3, 7, 4, 8; 3. 1, 5, 9, 2, 4, 8, 7, 3; 4. 5, 2, 9, 3, 8, 4, 1, 7; 5. 6, 5, 8, 2, 4, 1, 7, 3

Page 34

Page 35

1. 49 ÷ 7 = 7; 2. 18 ÷ 9 = 2; 3. 27 ÷ 9 = 3; 4. 24 ÷ 3 = 8; 5. 45 ÷ 5 = 9; 6. 40 ÷ 8 = 5; 7. 63 ÷ 7 = 9; 8. 36 ÷ 6 = 6; 9. 42 ÷ 7 = 6; 10. 48 ÷ 12 = 4; 11. 88 ÷ 11 = 8; 12. 40 ÷ 10 = 4

Page 36

1. 7; 2. 6; 3. 10; 4. 9; 5. 4; 6. 5; 7. 8; 8. 3; 9. 5; 10. 7; 11. 7; 12. 6; 13. 10; 14. 1; 15. 5; 16. 8; 17. 2; 18. 11

Answer: BECAUSE THEY FORGOT THE WORDS

Page 37

Page 38

1. 5 = 45 ÷ 9, 10 ÷ 2, 25 ÷ 5, 40 ÷ 8, 15 ÷ 3, and 30 ÷ 6; 2. 3 = 21 ÷ 7, 9 ÷ 3, 27 ÷ 9, 18 ÷ 6, 24 ÷ 8, 12 ÷ 4; 3. 8 = 64 ÷ 8, 8 ÷ 8 = 1, 72 ÷ 9, 56 ÷ 7, 48 ÷ 6, 32 ÷ 4; 4. 6 = 18 ÷ 3, 24 ÷ 4, 48 ÷ 8, 12 ÷ 2, 30 ÷ 5, 54 ÷ 9, 36 ÷ 6; 5. 2 = 12 ÷ 6, 16 ÷ 8, 6 ÷ 3, 14 ÷ 7, 10 ÷ 5, 8 ÷ 4, 18 ÷ 9

Page 39

Answer: A BED

Page 40

1. 4; 2. 9; 3. 6; 4. 9; 5. 6; 6. 7; 7. 9; 8. 7; 9. 7; 10. 8; 11. 3; 12. 6; 13. 10; 14. 4; 15. 9; 16. 8

Page 41

Page 42

Answer: ADDRESS

Page 43

Page 44

1. 36 ÷ 4 = 9; 2. 35 ÷ 5 = 7; 3. 15 ÷ 5 = 3; 4. 44 ÷ 11 = 4; 5. 24 ÷ 8 = 3; 6. 54 ÷ 6 = 9; 7. 35 ÷ 7 = 5; 8. 72 ÷ 9 = 8